Index

Page	Title and age of child in years	Thoughts behind each chapter
1	Introduction	Intended purpose of the book
3	Hello World! (0)	Baby's thoughts immediately after delivery
5	Look What I Can Do! (1)	Turning over and crawling
7	New Baby Time (2)	Spotlight sharing; Mommy pregnant
11	From Diapers To Wipers (3)	Potty training
13	Oh No! Not Again!! (4)	Mommy pregnant yet another time
15	Crudeness Is Rudeness (5)	Importance of practicing good manners
17	Golden Rule Time (6)	Treat others as you would like to be treated
19	Be Cool At School (7)	The excitement and importance of school
21	Love All Thy Fellow Munchkins Equally (8)	Embracing tolerance and rejecting bigotry
25	Each Of Us Is Special (9)	Loving a brother with Down Syndrome
27	Not Enough Hours (10)	Too many activities versus family time
31	I Think I'm Fine (11)	Dealing with disappointments in life
33	Don't Blush When Looking In The Mirror (12)	Body changes with adolescence
35	It's Teen Time (13)	Adjusting to being a teenager
39	Never Date A Meanie (14)	Choose your date wisely
41	One Tough Cookie! and Why Me? (15)	A friend dealing with childhood cancer
47	Act All Grown Up When Driving (16)	Learning to drive
51	Choices (17)	Resisting temptation and peer pressure
55	Can I Handle The Storms Without My Umbrella (18)	Leaving the protective nest of home
59	Conclusion	Lessons learned! On with a wonderful life!!

To order additional copies of this book, contact:
Xlibris
844-714-8691
www.Xlibris.com
Orders@Xlibris.com

ISBN: 978-1-6641-8261-5 (sc)
ISBN: 978-1-6641-8262-2 (hc)
ISBN: 978-1-6641-8260-8 (e)

Print information available on the last page

Rev. date: 04/23/2024

Dedicated First to my own parents:

Charles and Beatrice Marks

and

Second to all other parents;

Each of us, while possibly making mistakes along the way, strive
to do the best we can for those children in our charge, whose very
lives and futures we shape in ways we will never fully know.

and

Third to Marlene;

My stunning, adoring wife, and unparalleled mother; without whose caring and counsel
our children might not have turned into the wonderful parents they are today.

Introduction

Long ago the Lord did hand us
Ten things sacred, to command us
How to get along with others;
And to live our lives in peace.

Yet there are many who ignore His laws,
And bad guys who abhor His laws.
But mostly we're good people
Who are anxious to obey.

But what of those still growing?
Taught by parents to be knowing
Golden Rules; those parents showing
By example........right from wrong.

As they grow, these thoughts may guide them,
So you'll never wish to hide them
When some devilish streak inside them
Whispers, *"Don't play by the rules!"*

They'll ignore that nasty voice inside;
Ingrained to choose that choice inside
Their little brains that tell them
What is nice and what is not.

To help digest, absorb, and swallow
All suggestions that now follow,
Every stage of life will illustrate
The point each mandate makes.

From first breath to adolescent,
(Not all subjects wholly pleasant)
These few stories are a present:
They're a guide to life well lived.

Birth

Your own personal photos or treasured memories
As a new life begins

Hello World! (O)

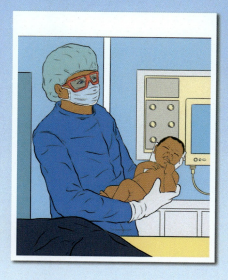

When first expanding lungs to scream
I looked in shock! *"Is this a dream?"*
I felt so warm, so wet; secure.
I was quite certain; knew for sure
I would have no need to endure
The world outside of Mommy!

Then suddenly, *"Plop!"*
And out I popped.
No sooner landed, I was handed
To some girl who *"Oohed and aahed."*

"Look, it's a boy," or *"It's a girl."*
I couldn't hear well, my head a whirl.
I was confused, but sure not bored;
Oh no! They're going to cut the cord!

It really did not hurt a bit.
I knew I shouldn't be such a twit.
But man, I sure had had it good.
If given choices I sure would
Have stayed inside forever........

But I had no choice at all!

Then before they wrapped me up in blankets,
Tush exposed...How cruel! They spanked it.
I cried so loud; I'll bet that got 'em!
I'll teach them to slap my bottom!

In hugs and kisses I was smothered.
Daddy daddied; Mommy mothered.
I knew that I had passed inspection;
Full intact; no odd infection.
In their eyes I was perfection!

They murmured lesson number one:
*"Be tough, my sweet girl; or my son.
As you well know, the cord's no longer.
You'll grow taller; bigger; stronger.
Life will throw you fastballs, curves;
You'll learn to duck, and dodge, and swerve."*

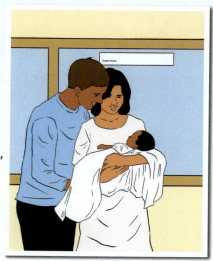

I yawned and napped; in no big hurry.
I'm fed; I'm warm. What's there to worry?

Age 1

Your own personal photos or treasured memories
At this stage of life

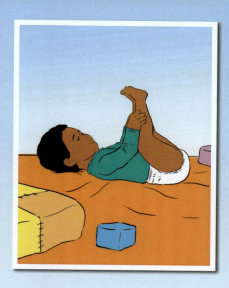

Look What I Can Do! (1)

There really wasn't much to do.
Just eat, and sleep, and burp, and poo;
And smile when I was coochie cooed,
Or frown if I didn't like the food.

They'd set me on my tummy,
Blankie squishing on my nose.
The carpet smelled like dog fur,
And like stinky socks and clothes.
They placed me tushie upwards, sighing
"What a darling pose!"
I was stuck there 'til the day I squirmed
And strugglingly arose
To roll from front to back!
Hurrah! I now could see my toes!

The day I first said *"Mama"*
I was barely six months old.
The way they carried on.........
You'd think I'd won Olympic gold!

And soon I spied my very
Extra favorite toy of all;
Way far across the room,
Laying cattywhampus by the wall.
The only way to get there? Muscle up!
I learned to crawl.

In weeks I walked; and soon I talked,
Advancing at full throttle.
Might I soon eat pizza?
Sure beats warm milk from the bottle.

Age 2

Your own personal photos or treasured memories
At this stage of life

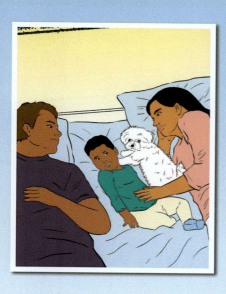

New Baby Time (2)

I've gone from crawl to walk to toddle:
You just watch and wait!
Now sippy cups! And no more bottle;
<u>Almost</u> steady gait!

I learn a new word every day now,
So much more that I can say now.
I crawl in bed, and snuggly lay now
Between my two best friends.
That's Mommy, and that's Daddy,
But there's one more in our group;
Our little puppy, Candy, but she knows she'd best not poop
On pillows or in blankets, 'cause it's gross to have to scoop
That yucky stuff from off the covers, if Candy made an "Oops."

But there's one thing that I can't figure.
Mommy sure is growing bigger.
Her feet aren't fat, no change in slippers;
She sure, though, cannot close her zippers.
There's some thing I've heard called a hip,
And hers is disappearing!

Most anything that you can mush, from peas to Brussel sprouts,
I'll drool and lick my little chops, but spinach I'll spit out!
I love those colored bears, all gummy;
Ice cream? Yum! And cookies? Nummy!
I know I'm small, but I'm no dummy;
It must have tasted awful crummy.
When Mommy gulped into her tummy
An itsy bitsy baby!

"Yes, there's a baby sis or brother.
Soon, my sweet, there'll be another
Little hungry mouth to mother,
Like I mothered you."

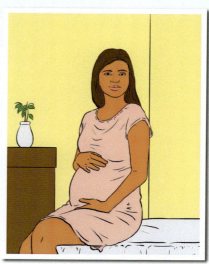

Age 2

Your own personal photos or treasured memories
At this stage of life

I somehow knew it didn't make sense.
Her tummy now was huge! Immense!
When I eat food, I stain my diapers.
Scream and cry, 'til I find wipers.
And nothing that I ever make
Looks anything like what I'd take
In to my arms to kiss, and hug.
I'd rather eat a French fried bug!

"A miracle, Divine creation."
Whatever! I'll just watch my station;
Nick For Kids, or Disney stuff;
Aw, come on guys; I beg – enough!
But....could there really be a baby
Living in your tummy? Maybe......

Wait a sec'. What's that thing kickin?
It couldn't be cake, or crispy chicken.
Nah! I'm sure there's some mistake.
'Cause how can *"water ever break?"*

"Hon; Grammy, Grandpa both will stay
With you tonight; you'll laugh and play,
While me and Daddy go away
To empty out my tummy!"

"Then we'll be back before you know.
Now give us kisses, as we go
To have a baby, and to <u>show</u> you
That's what was inside me!"

I knew that things were going to change;
My household status rearranged.
But one thing that I doubted never:
We'd love each other more than ever!

Age 3

Your own personal photos or treasured memories
At this stage of life

From Diapers To Wipers (3)

Next up: challenge harder yet;
More difficult to master.
Mistakes formed lakes, and muddy swamps;
And beans spelled pure disaster.
I'd have to move out super speed,
Get to the bathroom faster......
Before tummy said, *"too late!"*

Every baby who'd been walking
Babbling gibberish all day,
Stayed the center of attraction,
But tried hard to stay away
From that big white bowl
Where, *"I saw Mommy*
Sit one day and groan.
She made such terrible sounds;
I think she thought she was alone.
And Daddy too, makes noises,
But he doesn't move his mouth.
I think he's playing the tuba;
But the tunes come from the south!?"

"They don't seem too excited
When they sit, and seem to squeeze.
But I'm as happy as a clam;
Poop when and where I please."

But now they frown; say sternly, *"Baby,*
Don't say "No," or even "Maybe."
We both know, and so do you,
You are the boss of where you poo!"

I may be young, but I'm not dumb.
They'll bribe me soon, of course.
Perhaps I'll take a unicorn,
Or bouncy rocking horse.

We came to an agreement.
Poopy diapers were no more.
My butt was clean; and this would mean
No messes on the floor.

Age 4

Your own personal photos or treasured memories
At this stage of life

Oh No! Not Again!! (4)

I once had it all;
Center stage; one and only;
The solo attraction,
Not a teensy bit lonely.

How well I remember
How Mommy inflated;
And soon after that
How my role was downgraded.
I no longer felt quite as *app*reciated
When new baby brother arrived.

But then over time
I slowly adjusted.
My parents still loved me;
I totally trusted
I ranked number one.
But now I'm disgusted,
'Cause Mommy's inflating again!

I learned to adapt
When they brought home my brother.
But now I can see
There will soon be another.
And if you are asking
What would be my druthers?
I'd rather they left it at two!!

But there was no voting.
My parents are gloating
About their three kids; and it's obvious they're floating
Elated with joy on Cloud 9.
OK! If it must be so......fine!

Now I am cool with a new baby sister.
Until she was here I didn't know that I missed her.
And Mommy and Daddy assure me (in private)
I'll always be top of the heap!

Age 5

Your own personal photos or treasured memories
At this stage of life

Crudeness Is Rudeness (5)

Every munchkin now has playdates,
Has to get on well with others.
Impress their dads and siblings – yes -
But most important – mothers!
If a Mommy thinks, *"Bad influence!"*
She'll make it clear as day.
"You're free to talk at school,
But please go somewhere else to play!"

You never want to be that kid
Tossed out like stinky fish.
You want to be the one to whom
That Mommy brings a dish
Of her cookies: chocolate chip! Fresh baked!
Here's how to get that wish:

Show basic manners always; such as:
Cover mouth when burping.
Drink sodas, shakes, or cocoa,
But remember – there's no slurping!
Don't ever pick your nose,
Or if you must – be real discrete.
And never...ever...toot your tush
When someone's trying to eat.
Don't pick on baby brother;
Don't forget to flush the toilet.
Say please; and not saying thank you
Could still ruin the mood and spoil it.

By keeping all these things in mind
(Well mannered mouth, behaved behind),
One day, without a doubt, you'll find
More friends than you can count.

Age 6

Your own personal photos or treasured memories
At this stage of life

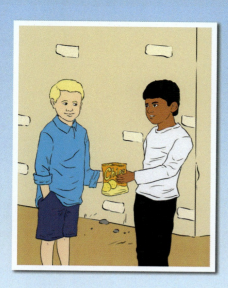

Golden Rule Time: Treat Others As You Would Like Them To Treat You (6)

We've mastered all the basics;
Not to spit, throw food, or shout.
Those lousy things that some kids do
To get them thrown out
Of places where to be polite
Is rightfully expected;
Where choices wrong
Are long since gone,
And utterly rejected.

Now how does one get in a group
So mannered and elite?
It always helps to wear clean socks,
And not have stinky feet.
To share with friends your yummy chips,
Or frosting covered treat.

If someone talks, don't interrupt;
Hear what they have to say.
If you're playing with someone smaller
Never grab their toy away.

When visiting, don't scribble walls;
Spill grape juice on the rug;
Stick boogers in the oatmeal,
Top your pancakes with a bug.

Don't pull the tail of your friend's dog,
Stick kitty in the toaster.
Let others say how good you are,
'Cause no one likes a boaster.

The list goes on;
The "Do's" and "Don'ts,"
What never should be done.
And you'll soon find you can behave;
And still have tons of fun!

Age 7

Your own personal photos or treasured memories
At this stage of life

Be Cool At School (7)

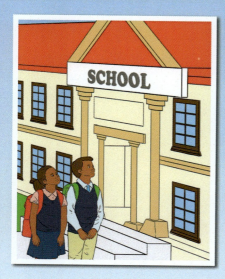

The school bell rings.
Did you just bring
All things that you might need?
Did Mommy pack a lunch to munch
And books you'll learn to read?
Did you remember undies,
And make sure to close your zipper?
Are you wearing shoes and socks,
Or still in your house slippers?

Of course, all checks out fine;
And now it's time to meet your teacher.
Will she cackle like a witch, and drool?
Some horrid, screaming creature?
Not even close. She's beautiful.........
"Miss Davis is my name.
We'll learn, we'll play; I love being here.
I hope you'll feel the same."

The kiddies loved her so! They listened.
No one ever dared
To tune her out – out of respect;
And not because they're scared.
They knew what she was teaching
They would need for all their lives.
When the tiny girls take husbands,
And the little guys take wives.

So they always paid attention,
And they never talked in class.
They learned to read, and learned to spell;
Had picnics on the grass.
They learned their mathematics,
And were taught about the world.
They felt the pride and knew The Pledge
When our flag was unfurled.

Like sponges they absorbed
The many things she had to teach them
By granting the respect she'd earned.
She'd shown she could reach them,
And taught them well! Under her spell
They learned to read and write.
And the wondrous tales she read them
Gave them wondrous dreams each night!

Age 8

Your own personal photos or treasured memories
At this stage of life

Love All Thy Fellow Munchkins Equally (8)

In school we learn about the world;
What makes it rain or snow.
What makes a jet plane fast,
And how short legs make turtles slow.
We see in different countries
How some people talk or dress.
We try to draw, and try to paint;
Which sure can make a mess.
We don't pay much attention
To who sits across the row.
Don't care if her art's good or bad,
Or if he's fast or slow.
And truly couldn't care less; I think
We may not even know
If he's a she, or she's a he.
Those things don't matter. So………

Why do bullies on the playground push and shove,
And try to boss?
Say nasty things like, "Tell me, creep,
Explain: I'm at a loss
To why you're friends with
Every loser that you come across?
Including those with skin
Way different color than your own?
Or all those kids with accents
Who you surely know have grown
With parents fresh from who knows where?
I've noticed, 'cause you've shown
Your friendship for that long named kid,
Whose father wears a turban.
And that girl they say
Has "special needs!"
She sure don't mind disturbin'
The rest of us in class all day;
I'll tell you that it's sure been
Goofy watching you befriend
Most everyone you meet.
Like that guy who walks all funny,
And has braces on his feet.

Age 8

Your own personal photos or treasured memories
At this stage of life

You hang out with all those weirdo kids
Who never even go
To the one and only church that counts;
But why? I'm sure you know
That any faith besides my own
Does absolutely blow!"

_____

Who hates such as this?
Had this bully been soured
By parents who taught him,
And thoroughly scoured
Kind thoughts fully out of his head?

Whatever!

But those words with which he'd showered me
Had emboldened and empowered me.
Smugly thought I was a coward. Me?

I said what he needed to hear!!

"I can't believe you're such a jerk!
All people are the same.
We're all made by a loving God,
It's really such a shame
That you have not seen for yourself
There's not one right or wrong.
We all do march to different tunes,
And favor different songs.
Some day you'll be much happier
If you learn to get along!!"

Age 9

Your own personal photos or treasured memories
At this stage of life

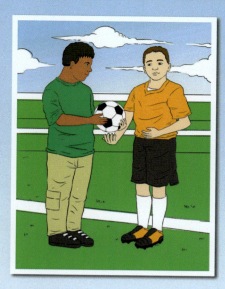

Each Of Us Is Special (9)

While some of us have been denied
What most will take for granted,
It's clear as day that for those kids
The playing field has been slanted.

My brother's always smiling,
And he'll always share his toys.
He's sweet to all our girl friends,
And he never bullies boys.
He never is demanding,
And you know he'll wait his turn;
With kindness and with warmth
He has absolutely earned
A special place in our hearts.

He has a syndrome they call "Down,"
And some at school poke fun.
Yes he talks somewhat differently,
Is awkward when he runs.
But there's much more to life
Than being the best guy on the team.
We each have different goals to reach;
We each have different dreams.
My brother doesn't strive to be
An astronaut, or teacher;
A doctor, or a lawyer,
But you'll never find a creature
On G-d's green earth whose nature
Is so giving, so serene.
Whose DNA says "No" to genius,
But also "No" to mean.

Perhaps kids like my brother
Have been put here for a reason;
To teach us – unlike sports-
There's no one specific season
To accept we all are different,
And we each, in our own way
Can make our world a better place
Than how it is today.

Age 10

Your own personal photos or treasured memories
At this stage of life

Not Enough Hours (10)

Each of us is born with skills
That come with human genes.
To what, exactly, then
Do all of us possess the means
To do, or say, or function?
Or do our genes just not mean beans?

Not all, but most of us
Were blessed
To smell, and speak, and hear;
Determine with our sense of touch and sight
What's far or near.
Our inner sense directs us
When to welcome, when to fear.

But other than anatomy,
What difference: Rae from Ricky?
Yes, one may be accepting;
Or another may be picky.....
But moreso, it's our special skills;
And that's where it gets tricky!!

Some Daddies are heard telling sons,
"Without sports you're a zero.
Become a jock, my boy,
And you'll be hailed as a hero."

It all begins with soccer.
"Time to learn to kick a ball."
Karate, baseball, swimming;
Then comes football in the fall.

Lots of Mommies tell their girls
The benefits of sports.
While fitting them in jerseys
And their sport specific shorts,
They'll frequently add to that list
Activities less rough;
For instance, cheer, and dancing;
But as if that weren't enough.....

Age 10

Your own personal photos or treasured memories
At this stage of life

"It's both your mind and body
To which you must pay attention.
So, getting home from soccer camp,
Have we forgot to mention
That your piano teacher's waiting?
Now be careful, dear; you're drenchin'
The piano bench with sweat;
But that's OK, you'll hear no shouting;
'Cause after wolfing dinner down
We'll drop you off at scouting."

"And then it's time for homework;
Then it's time to get to bed.
I think you have a test tomorrow,
And sleep will clear your head."

"Stop!"

Every hour – dawn 'til dusk –
Is totally directed!
I may be gifted, may be not;
But this should be expected:
Some time for us to laugh and hug.......
Take care we've not selected
A schedule too demanding.
We can never leave neglected
The closeness of our family.
That must always be protected!

Age 11

Your own personal photos or treasured memories
At this stage of life

I Think I'm Fine (11)

My friend, Michelle,
Is not so well;
Her Dad is moving out!
At least it will be quiet;
"They would always scream and shout."

And my friend Tommy said
"They had to put my dog to sleep."
It hurt me to see Tommy, as he told me,
Start to weep.

My cousin in Milwaukee called
With grief she couldn't hide.
She'd never see her Gramps again.
She couldn't believe he died!

And what of me? I heard last night
My parents started yelling.
I feared the worst:
They'd walk in to my room,
While sadly telling:
"Dear, this is it!
It's time to quit."
Not buying what each was selling.
But no! Their fight was all about
The fact the trash was not put out!
And now we'd have to bear a week
Of stinky fish and sauerkraut!

"How long will our sweet puppy live?"
My parents then explained,
"Their lifetimes aren't as long as ours, dear;
One day she'll be drained
Of every drop of energy, but that's a long ways off.
For now let's fend off heartworm,
Fleas and ticks, and kennel cough."

My Grandpa's live and kickin';
He and Grammy swing and jive.
I'm glad to say the both of them
Are very much alive!

Sometimes in everybody's life
There's disappointment; sadness.
But mostly, with a little luck,
It's overwhelmed by gladness!!

Age 12

Your own personal photos or treasured memories
At this stage of life

Don't Blush When Looking In The Mirror (12)

You've learned how not
To burp in public,
Listen well in school.
Give everyone an equal chance;
Apply the Golden rule.
But never were you ever taught
To welcome, not to fear
The changes that you see
When you stand staring in the mirror!

You've now reached adolescence;
Girls might marvel, *"Look at those!"*
And whether you're a girl or boy -
"What? Pimples on my nose?"

Now suddenly there's hair
In places yesterday smooth skin.
*"My armpits smell like pond scum,
And I never seem to win
Those battles fought with razors
On my legs, or face, or pits.
I try to hide – just out of pride -
Those multiplying zits!"*

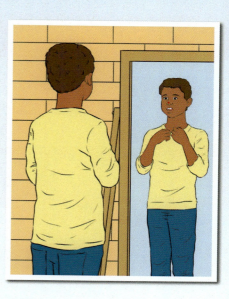

*"With shoes too small
I'm off the wall;
Mood swings you wouldn't believe.
I wanted to grow up, but now I simply stare and grieve
For the kid I was just yesterday."* But age goes just one way:
In one direction; forward. We can try, but cannot stay
The bouncing teensy babies, shielded from what isn't nice.
It's time to take more seriously our parents' sage advice:
*"Accept the changes gracefully; you'll be glad one day they came.
One basic law of nature: Nothing ever stays the same!"*

Age 13

Your own personal photos or treasured memories
At this stage of life

It's Teen Time (13)

I'm sort of getting used to this:
I don't look quite the same.
They say, *"You're growing like a weed!*
And filling out your frame."

But that's not all.
If growing tall
Were all these teen years meant,
I'd count that as a blessing;
As a gift, from Heaven sent!

See...As a girl
I ask my Mom
When some things don't seem right:
"What should I do?
She sends Dad to the pharmacy
That night.

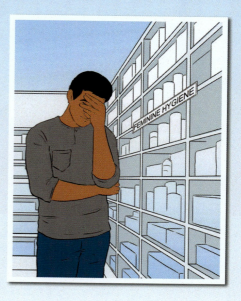

And, as a guy
I hear my voice
Has horrible changing tones.
It may sound like a piccolo
Or like a bass trombone.

My friends are seeming to divide;
Some jock-like, others nerdy.
Some come to school all neat and prim,
Some come unkempt and dirty.
There's cliques, there's hicks,
There's "cools," there's fools;
There's teacher's pets and punks.
One wants to be a doctor;
And another be a monk!

It's hard not to be influenced;
It's tough not to be tempted.
To ignore the lure of others;
To be totally exempted
From joining groups, or even gangs;
But then I think of when
My parents taught me right from wrong,
And then I think again:

Age 13

Your own personal photos or treasured memories
At this stage of life

Exteriors may be changing.
I look different as a whole.
But I've got strength of spirit,
Resolution in my soul.

So I'll just stay myself;
I won't commit to any bunch.
Share friendships with those wishing such.
With needy – share my lunch.

Age 14

Your own personal photos or treasured memories
At this stage of life

Never Date A Meanie (14)

With all those changes that I see
With bodily review,
I just don't feel attractive.
I'd think others think that too.
But clearly I am wrong,
Because I've noted that of late
The kids I thought were simply friends
Are asking for a date!

My dad says, *"Son, be careful.*
Girls will make your logic melt!"
To girls, advice is different;
Said with caution; deeply felt.
"Be careful, sweetie. I know guys.
They try to prove they're cool.
Remember what we've taught you,
And the lessons learned in school."

But whether boys or girls, *"Be sure*
They're just as nice as you.
Perhaps a Disney movie,
Or share popcorn at the zoo."

"A pizza, or a burger;
Try to be back home by ten.
And if they treat you well enough,
You might go out again."

"In any case, choose wisely;
You deserve the very best.
Date only those who put you first;
And discard all the rest."

Age 15

Your own personal photos or treasured memories
At this stage of life

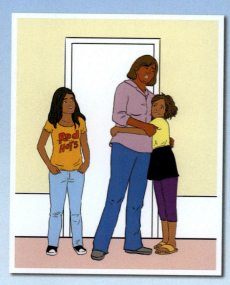

One Tough Cookie! (15)

The pitcher on our softball team
Seemed healthy as a horse.
In blazing sun, or soaking rain,
She'd always stay the course.

Until the day she didn't show up.
Our coach gave us the answer:
Next up at bat? A slugger cruel!
"She's trying to strike out cancer!"

I called her Mom.
*"Come visit, dear.
So, how's the team without her?
She gave us quite a scare, you know,
But never did we doubt her
Strength and resolve!"*

I rang the bell.
"You look just swell!"
Not so......but what I said.
Her face had tightened,
Skin had lightened;
A new "do" topped her head.

I knew it could have been much worse.
We hugged; she asked what's new.
And then she handed me a poem.
*"Please share my point of view:
This tells others who may face the same
Exactly how I felt.
It's not what I signed up for,
But you play the cards you're dealt."*

I read her words "**Why Me?**"
And wept;
Imaging her plight.
I pass this story
On to you;
Of her heroic fight.....

If your family or someone dear to you has been impacted by this or some other devastating disease or condition, consider adding your own personal photos or memories.

Why Me?

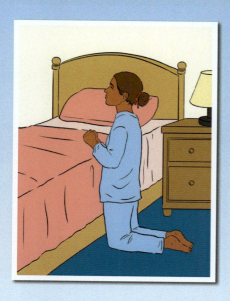

There's no way we can ever know
The plans He's made for us, and so
We praise Him, and with bended knee
We look to Heaven; wait and see
What fate awaits both you and me.
For never will we find the answer
To the question, *"Why me? Cancer?"*

The school year's ending. It's vacation!
Time to watch the Disney station
All day long; or maybe campouts.
Who cares if it's hot or damp out?
It's later when we put the lamp out.

Maybe car trips, since it's summer.
But I feel sort of weak – a bummer!
The doctor said *"I think it best
If we run just a few more tests."*

Then suddenly everything was changed;
All upside down, and rearranged.
My parents hugged me tight, and cried;
No difference of how hard they tried
They shook, and trembled from inside.
I knew this wasn't good!

The next few weeks I sure didn't like.
I'd rather hike, or ride my bike.
Instead, Oh no! A needle? Yikes!
This wasn't fun at all!

This isn't what I would have chosen.
I wanted to, again, watch *Frozen*.
Who thought I'd be getting chemo
Instead of helping finding Nemo?
How could I be a princess fair
If I no longer had my hair?
Or be a prince – all strong and tough?
"Oh God! Please stop! I've had enough!!!!"

When I thought I could take no more,
My arms were bruised, my butt was sore,
A gentle *"Knock, knock,"* on the door;
The doctor entered – smiling!

If your family or someone dear to you has been impacted by this or some other devastating disease or condition, consider adding your own personal photos or memories.

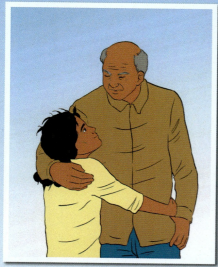

"I hesitate to use the word;
With cancer, it is never cured.
But go on home, and be assured
This battle's done. We've won!!"

Then time at home. As I recovered,
Mommy hugged, and Grammy hovered.
My hair grew back – both long and curly.
Daddy came home from work early;
Seemed all good, but I knew surely
This really wasn't normal.

But normal came back soon enough.
My Grandpa said, *"My gosh, you're tough!"*
The mirror I looked in said *"He's right!'*
And though I'd fought one nasty fight,
I felt, I saw, now I was quite
Back to where I started!

I hope these words encourage others;
Sisters, brothers, fathers, mothers.
If ever they are forced to hear
Those dreaded words; disease we fear.

Because.........

There's no way we can ever know
The plans He's made for us, and so
We praise Him, and with bended knee
We look to Heaven; wait and see
What fate awaits both you and me.
For never will we find the answer
To the question, *"Why me? Cancer?"*

Age 16

Your own personal photos or treasured memories
At this stage of life

Act All Grown Up When Driving (16)

In a sprawling 'burb of Texas
Cool young Jada drove her Lexus
In a manner that affects us
Really not so well at all!

She was constantly perplexing
Just why people felt that texting
Was a thing that really shouldn't be done
At all when driving cars.

She had earphones in her ears;
Felt that ample use of mirrors
Would negate her every fear
Of being bashed from side or rear.

And when staring at a graphic
On her phone, in heavy traffic
She felt fully in control;
Not an inattentive troll.

But she needed both her hands;
Because a phone - plus car - commands
That all limbs must move in tandem;
Movements cannot be just random.
Yet she suddenly felt a phantom
Prickly itching on her back!

There was nothing she could scratch with,
And that fearsome itch could match with
The very extra worst
That anyone could conjure up.

She pulled over to the side;
This she could not take in stride.
Then she ducked down low to hide
The fact she'd taken off her shirt!

What she saw was most appalling;
Something teensy, black; and crawling?
Seemed to lick its chops; 'twas stalling?
Waiting patiently, not falling
For the trick of being deprived
Of its meal: young Jada's hide!

Age 16

Your own personal photos or treasured memories
At this stage of life

More impetuous than foolish
Jada then did something ghoulish;
Clever? Yes! Beyond a doubt;
Wore her blouse turned inside out!

She sped home with i-tunes muted;
If behind a slow car? Tooted!
Thus her horn was loudly blaring,
Yet she was not one bit caring,
And was therefore very daring
In her race to get back home.

She whisked in through her front door;
Concerned parents she ignored.
As she peeled her itchy blouse away,
And flung it to the floor.

Then she gave it close inspection;
Used Dad's glasses for detection,
Thought she saw it with perfection;
That this bug was – yuck – a louse!

"OMG, how in my blouse
Did such a mean and vicious louse
Consider me his house
To set up shop and graze?
Did it crawl out from my hair?
Or come flying out from the air?
Where had been this louse's lair
Before settling on my back?"

Then she focused from confusion
With an ultimate conclusion:
She'd been under a delusion....
This was not a louse at all!

A piece of dirt was all it was;
A little tiny hairy fuzz!
The crazy way that Jada acted
Was because she'd been distracted,
And could have easily exacted
Ultra bad results!

So keep in mind to those who read this:
Don't ignore; take note and heed this:
Pat attention when you drive,
And help us all to stay alive!!

Age 17

Your own personal photos or treasured memories
At this stage of life

Choices (17)

Now I can drive. Feel so alive!
I sure can flex my muscle.
Like cars, some things can go too fast;
Should I slow down the hustle?

A junior now; just one more year,
And I'll be free at last.
From parents' supervision,
And the way they always cast
Those looks that say,
"I think you shouldn't"
Or *"Absolutely no!"*
I should be glad.....Right?
But I'm not! Their words have helped me grow
The spine to challenge bad peers, who encourage me to go
To dark and scary places!

*"Hey, it's OK. It's only weed.
What harm? Just take a puff!
It might just make you mellow, man;
Relax you just enough
To say, "That's cool! I've been a fool
For saying "No" all these years.
In looking back you'd know
It made no sense to have those fears."*

*"And booze, wow! Just a couple shots
Your head will spin around.
Not hard to get; when parents leave
I've snooped around and found
A whole supply, of which I'm sure
They hardly keep a count
Of just how many beers are stored;
Or gin, in what amount."*

*"And we heard that on dates
You really care with whom you're kissing.
I think that you should loosen up,
And see what you've been missing."*

Age 17

Your own personal photos or treasured memories
At this stage of life

It's creeps like those
Who say they're friends
From whom I walk away;
I think they really do all of those
Bad things that they say
Are "*cool*," and "*in*,"
But I know there will sometime come a day
When those who've lived their lives too fast
Will have a price to pay.
So thank you, Mommy,
Thank you Dad.
I bow my head and pray....

That never will I forget the lessons you have taught me.

Age 18

Your own personal photos or treasured memories
At this stage of life

Can I Handle The Storms Without My Umbrella? (18)

I'm graduating high school; this fall headed off to college.
But do I have the moral strength, the fortitude, and knowledge
To tell what's right from wrong, and not say *"yes"* when I mean *"no?"*
To look temptation in the eye, and tell it, *"You can go*
To take a hike! And don't come back! I think you really blow!"
I think I do. I'm strong. I know you reap just what you sow.

My parents (both by wisdom and example) now have taught me
To choose the straight and narrow path, and more than once have caught me
As I began to stray off course. They've shown, and I've learned
Respect for elders and for peers is not assumed – but earned.

The water's deep, and cold;
Am I prepared to dive head first
Into what I've been told
Can be the best, or be the worst?
So far I've been protected;
Not experienced, just rehearsed
What life is really like out there.
Now will my bubble burst?
My life's been thus far blessed;
Now will it suddenly be cursed?

Age 18

Your own personal photos or treasured memories
At this stage of life

There ain't no way!!!
My moral code is solid as a rock!
It's built from love, and guidance from Above,
So I've a lock
In both my heart and soul, of when to listen, and to whom.
My compass is unwavering. There simply is no room
To call the *"glass half empty,"* or to think of gloom and doom.
And all I've learned since first I shivered, popping from the womb
Has made me who I am today; a woman strong and proud;
A man whose courage and conviction stands out from the crowd.
I treasure all you've taught me, and if asked I'd shout it loud,
"You've always had my back, and it's with certainty I say,
My deepest thanks; you've made me into who I am today."

With tears it's time to say good bye;
To leave my nurtured nest;
Where first I saw the light of day,
While you, who love me best,
Shed tears yourselves, and think of all together we've been through.
Forever will you be beloved by me, and me by you.......

Your own personal photos or treasured memories
As your children continue to explore
Their own paths through life

Conclusion

Now if never you abandon
What you've read herein, demandin'
You to always care for others
Like you'd have them care for you.....

Then with manners full enlightened,
And your social polish brightened,
Grip on couth forever tightened;
You'll have no cause to be frightened
That you won't always be loved.
Not just by parents – dear since birth with you –
But all who share this earth with you!

People's awe for you will mount;
With more friends than you can count.
If you keep these basic points in mind
You'll be one cool, cool, cat!

Your own personal photos or treasured memories
As your children continue to explore
Their own paths through life.

Your own personal photos or treasured memories
As your children continue to explore
Their own paths through life.